THE HIGH SCHOOL
SPORTS
PARENT

Developing Triple-Impact Competitors

By Jim Thompson

BALANCE SPORTS
PUBLISHING

Balance Sports Publishing, LLC · Portola Valley, California

Balance Sports Publishing, LLC
195 Lucero Way
Portola Valley, CA 94028
(650) 561-9586

LIBRARY OF CONGRESS CATALOG-IN-PRINTING DATA
Thompson, Jim, 1949-
        The high school sports parent : developing triple-impact competitors /
by Jim Thompson. — 1st ed.

        p. ; cm.

        ISBN: 978-0-9821317-3-2

1. School sports—Psychological aspects. 2. Parent and teenager. 3. High school athletes—Family relationships. I. Title.

GV709.2 .T56 2009
796/.042

FIRST EDITION
Printed in the United States of America

10 9 8 7 6 5 4 3   13 12

Designed by Elisa Tanaka

Cover photo by Jill Carmel

A special thank you to Laura and Gary Lauder for their encouragement and financial support of this book.

Deep appreciation to the "brain trust" of high school coaches, athletic directors, and parents that helped inform this book: Doug Abrams, Dr. Casey Cooper, Jeaney Garcia, Ken Harkenrider, Molly Hellerman, Steve Henderson, Janet Holdsworth, Dann Jacobson, Ray Lokar, Rose Lowe, Rosie Martinez, Patrick McCrystle, Dan McGee, Dave Parsh, Jim Perry, Jason Sacks, Tina Syer, Mike Terborg, and Kathy Toon.

Table of Contents

Table of Contents *continued*

Preface

I've had three shots at high school sports – as athlete (a pretty long time ago!), sports parent, and coach. Each time I felt unprepared to successfully negotiate a dizzying experience that felt so important.

Because high school sports has huge symbolic meaning in our society, and because it roosts in our memory for a lifetime, there is often regret.

That regret – "I could have done so much better with high school sports if only I had known more" – powers much of my work with Positive Coaching Alliance and, in particular, this book.

It's said that we need to learn from our mistakes, but wouldn't it be great sometimes to learn from someone else's mistakes!

The experience of many parents, coaches, athletic directors, and athletes (and especially Jim Lobdell, Steve Seely, and Colleen Anderson at Balance Sports Publishing) who are all part of the PCA Movement informs this book. This deep pool of experience provides a framework and powerful, practical tools you can use to help your teen thrive in high school sports. So you won't have to repeat the mistakes we made.

This is all part of achieving the mission of Positive Coaching Alliance to transform youth sports so sports can transform youth. PCA's goal is to change the culture of youth and high school sports so every

- Coach is a **Double-Goal Coach®** who prepares athletes to win and teaches life lessons through sports

- Athlete aspires to be a **Triple-Impact Competitor™** who makes self, teammates, and the game better

- Sports parent becomes a **Second-Goal Parent**™ who concentrates on their child's character development while letting athletes and coaches focus on the first goal of winning on the scoreboard

This vision is shared by a growing number of prominent coaches, athletes, and youth sports experts who comprise PCA's National Advisory Board, including:

Jennifer Azzi, Olympic gold medalist, Basketball

Shane Battier, Houston Rockets

Larry Brown, Hall of Fame Basketball Coach

Nadia Comaneci, Olympic gold medalist, Gymnastics

Bart Conner, Olympic gold medalist, Gymnastics

Joan Duda, Sports Psychology, University of Birmingham, England

Carol Dweck, Author of *Mindset: The New Psychology of Success*

Joe Ehrmann, Founder, Building Men and Women for Others

Joy Fawcett, Olympic gold medalist, Soccer

Howard Gardner, Harvard Graduate School of Education

Chip Heath, Co-Author of *Made to Stick*

Phil Jackson, Head Coach, Los Angeles Lakers

Ronnie Lott, Hall of Fame Football Player

Dot Richardson, Olympic gold medalist, Softball

Doc Rivers, Head Coach, Boston Celtics

Summer Sanders, Olympic gold medalist, Swimming

Dean Smith, Hall of Fame Basketball Coach

The High School Sports Parent is intended to help you make wise use of the swiftly passing time you have as a parent of a high school athlete, so you won't have as many regrets as I have. That is my wish for you and your family.

Jim Thompson
Founder and Executive Director
Positive Coaching Alliance
www.PositiveCoach.org

CHAPTER ONE

The Second-Goal Parent: A Focus on the Big Picture

I have long been a fan of "The Family Circus" comic strip. Perhaps my favorite strip of all time features the family dog barking up a storm in the middle of the night. Dad, irritated that he's been awakened from a much-needed sleep, clomps down the stairs to yell at Barfy, who dutifully hangs his head. Dad climbs back up the stairs while the cartoonist has a surprise for us. He pans back so we see in the far corner of the yard a burglar retreating.

We who see the "Big Picture" know Barfy has protected his family from a burglary. The dad, seeing only the "Little Picture," is angry at being disturbed.

This comic strip can serve as a metaphor for youth and high school sports. High school coaches and parents are often overwhelmed by so many Little Pictures filled with barking dogs that they miss the Big Picture entirely. How our teens do in any given sporting event is Little Picture. Whether they win or lose, play well or badly, laugh or cry after the game – all Little Picture.

What young people take away from high school sports to help them become successful, contributing members of society is the Big Picture. Whether they remain physically active throughout life, recognize the rewards of commitment and delayed gratification, learn to bounce back from difficulties with renewed determination, discover how to support other people within a team context – these are the Big Picture.

The Big Picture and You

This book describes a model of sports parenting that focuses relentlessly on the Big Picture. We call it the Second-Goal Parent.

There are two broad goals in high school sports: striving to win and building character so young people develop into successful, contributing members of society.

As important as winning is, Second-Goal Parents let coaches and athletes worry about the first goal of scoreboard results. *Second-Goal Parents have a much more important role to play: ensuring their sons and daughters take away from sports lessons that will help them be successful in life.* Remember, that is the Big Picture. And attending to this is much more vital than being an extraneous back-seat coach.

Of course there is nothing wrong with caring about whether your kid's team wins or loses. Go ahead and care about it! But the lifelong impact you can have – that no one else can in quite the way you can – is on the life lessons your son or daughter takes away from the high school sports experience. No one can be there for your athlete in this way better than you. No one.

If you embrace your role as a Second-Goal Parent, it will transform the way you see high school sports. It will help you act to seize the teachable moments that will come your way again and again because you are looking for them.

What might have seemed like a disappointing loss or a failure by your son or daughter becomes an opportunity to reinforce resiliency. A tough competition in forbiddingly hot, cold, or nasty weather can prompt a conversation with your teen about learning to enjoy challenges. Whether your athlete succeeds or fails on the playing field, you will be able to use the experiences to reinforce the kind of person you want him or her to be.

Honing a Second-Goal Focus

Let's say your son or daughter has just had an opportunity to make the winning play in a game and blew it. If you played the sport (perhaps even if you didn't), you may have suggestions for how they could have improved their play. We call this a "First-Goal focus" because it concentrates on helping the athlete do well on the scoreboard, which the larger sports culture always puts first.

My two decades of experience working with high school parents has taught me that First-Goal suggestions from parents are often not well received by their child. Athletes get so much coaching already – from coaches, from teammates, from the game itself. When parents add to this flood of coaching, it often overwhelms the athlete, like the proverbial straw that breaks the camel's back.

Instead of being a back-seat coach, hone a Second-Goal focus with your son or daughter. Rather than obsessing about the skills and strategy of the game, engage your teen around the life lessons that sports teach.

For example, on the car ride home after a game, focus on the Second Goal. Use questions and your own assertions (sparingly).

Questions

- "What did you learn from that experience?"

- "What was it like playing with the big game pressure?"

- "What about the game can you feel good about even though you lost?"

Assertions

- "I know in my life that I learn more from my failures than from my successes. In fact, times I've been successful have usually come from learning from my mistakes."

- "I'm proud of the way you dealt with the pressure at the end of the game. Many people get so afraid under pressure that they don't give their best effort. You didn't make the play, but you gave it a good shot!"

- "Resilience is such an important attribute. I love to see you bounce back after a disappointment."

Back to the Big Picture

The signature act of a Second-Goal Parent is relentlessly keeping one's eye on the Big Picture. Second-Goal Parents hear the barking dogs but don't allow themselves to get distracted from their goal of ensuring their children get the most from their high school sports experience. They develop a "muscle" that allows them to focus on the Big Picture even when others are freaking out over a First-Goal issue like an official's bad call.

I know from personal experience how hard this is. My hope for this book is that it will inspire and help you become a Second-Goal Parent with an eye on the Big Picture so your kid can have the very best sports experience possible.

Chapter 1 Take-Aways

1 Adults in high school sports too often get caught up in the Little Picture (performance on the field) and lose sight of the Big Picture (life lessons learned on the field).

2 There are two broad goals in high school sports: striving to win and building character so teens develop into happy, productive, contributing members of society.

3 Second-Goal Parents let coaches and athletes worry about winning. Parents have a much more important role: focusing on teachable moments and the life lessons that their kids can take away from sports.

CHAPTER TWO

The Triple-Impact Competitor:
A Higher Calling for High School Athletes

As a kid, I aspired to play center field for the New York Yankees. I threw a ball against the back wall of Our Savior's Lutheran Church in Colfax, North Dakota, hour after hour, day after day, imagining myself patrolling the Yankee Stadium outfield making amazing catches and cutting runners off at home.

Even way back then the siren song of professional sports was strong in the minds of youth athletes like me, calling me to be like Mickey (Mantle).

And that siren song has only gotten louder. Professional sports and the 24/7 media that feed off each other wield enormous influence over the aspirations of high school athletes.

How High School Sports Differs From Professional Sports

Professional sports is a business whose goal is making a profit by entertaining fans. That usually requires a winning team, which leads to a win-at-all-cost mentality. Unfortunately, professional sports and the media surrounding it have become powerful to the point that high school sports too often mimics professional sports.

Because the playing surfaces, rules, and equipment are similar for professional and high school sports, people tend to confuse them, especially since press coverage and fan interest are similar for both. But they are fundamentally different enterprises. High school sports is about developing outstanding people – that's the Big Picture! The scoreboard is a powerful tool for helping that happen, not an end in itself.

Unfortunately, many adults have lost sight of the Big Picture of high school sports and instead default to the win-at-all-cost mentality prevalent in professional sports. If you attend high school sports events, sooner or later you'll see adults – coaches and parents – stomping, yelling, and even fighting about Little Picture issues like playing time or an official's bad call.

By contrast, when high school sports are done right, coaches and parents work together to develop character traits and positive memories that student-athletes carry with them long after scores are forgotten.

Given the power of professional sports, it is normal for high school athletes to aspire to be like professional athletes, but it's not always healthy in the absence of a positive context for those aspirations.

A Higher Calling for High School Athletes

For most high school athletes, being an athlete makes up a huge part of their identity. Being on the high school team carries with it status and purpose at a time when an adolescent's life may seem just a little bit out of control.

The problem is that youth athletes too often focus on a flawed and incomplete notion of all that one could aspire to be in sports and life.

Conventionally people focus on athleticism and on an athlete as someone who is fast and powerful, able to do physical tasks required to excel in the game of his choice. So it is not unusual for a high school athlete to assume that physical ability is key and that being a great athlete is what he should aspire to.

Absent any other strong influence, high school athletes will set their sights low and emulate professional athletes. But there is a higher aspiration possible, and you can help your athlete reach for it. PCA has developed the model of the Triple-Impact Competitor who makes himself, his teammates, and the game better.

The Triple-Impact Competitor

Your child will not always win, but she can compete well in every game. Learning to compete well is an important life skill. The traits inherent in the Triple-Impact Competitor model – hard work, a teachable spirit, teamwork, leadership, respect – will help your athlete in sports, but even more in life.

The Triple-Impact Competitor is the highest form of competitor because he makes: 1) himself better, 2) his teammates better, and 3) the game better.

Triple-Impact Competitors have a "teachable spirit." They work extremely hard to get better, but they focus on personal mastery and improvement rather than simply trying to win on the scoreboard (more about this in Chapter 6). They strive to excel and see winning on the scoreboard as a by-product of their relentless march toward mastery.

Triple-Impact Competitors also constantly look for ways to make their team and teammates successful. Where an ego-centered athlete looks for a supporting cast to make herself look good, a Triple-Impact Competitor looks to help teammates become better and more productive. This is the essence of leadership and teamwork, on the playing field and in life.

The third level may be the most important for our society. A Triple-Impact Competitor makes the game itself better. He competes hard to win, but by a code of Honoring the Game, and would rather lose than win dishonorably (more on this in Chapter 8).

There is a very important advantage for an athlete who is able to internalize an identity as a Triple-Impact Competitor. When she fails or struggles, she can still feel a sense of satisfaction from working at all three levels that can sustain her in hard times.

There is very little encouragement and support in our current professional sports culture for high school athletes to become Triple-Impact Competitors. If a player helps a teammate score a goal, the goal scorer gets the lion's share of the recognition. Linemen who protect the quarterback rarely emerge from the background after a touchdown catch in the end zone. And boorish behavior, showboating, and even criminal activity may be tolerated as long as athletes perform well on the field.

You, as a Second-Goal Parent, can encourage your athlete to aspire to become a Triple-Impact Competitor, regardless of the kind of coaching he gets. But the ideal situation is a coach who shares that goal.

The Double-Goal Coach

A discussion of the qualities of a great high school coach would require an entire book. But one central idea is critical. High school coaches should be character educators.

A Double-Goal Coach uses sports to teach life lessons while preparing athletes to succeed on the scoreboard – always on the lookout for the teachable moment in whatever happens on the field, positive or negative.

Double-Goal Coaches always work hard to prepare their team to win (first goal), but they never sacrifice the second goal of character development merely to win a game or even a championship. They realize there is simply no better place to build character than on the playing field, and they see their goal as developing Triple-Impact Competitors.

High school coaches who measure themselves only by the scoreboard waste the endless procession of teachable moments that sports provide. Regrettably, way too many of them do. That's why PCA works so hard to promote Double-Goal Coaching through its workshops for youth and high school coaches throughout the country.

No matter how your teen's coaches coach, you can still help her have a great sports experience by acting on what you have already learned about being a Second-Goal Parent. If your coach seems to focus exclusively on the scoreboard, your role as Second-Goal Parent becomes even more important.

What You Can Do

Here are ways you can help your athlete understand what it means to be a Triple-Impact Competitor.

Introduce the concept. "I read about this idea of the Triple-Impact Competitor who makes himself better, his teammates better and the game better, and I thought of you."

Provide information. Give your athlete my book, *Becoming a Triple-Impact Competitor,* which is written specifically for high school athletes and can be ordered on the PCA web site (www.positivecoach.org).

Engage in conversation. Ask your child what he thinks about the Triple-Impact Competitor model. Point out examples of Triple-Impact Competitors you see in college or professional sports. Ask him if there is anyone he has played with who is a Triple-Impact Competitor.

Imagine what the world would be like if high schools were graduating thousands of Triple-Impact Competitors every year. And it can all start with you as a Second-Goal Parent who encourages your athlete to be a Triple-Impact Competitor.

Chapter 2 Take-Aways

1   High school sports is a fundamentally different enterprise than professional sports, an entertainment business in which winning on the scoreboard is paramount. High school sports is about developing great people.

2   The highest form of athlete is the Triple-Impact Competitor who 1) strives for personal mastery and improvement, 2) looks for ways to make his team and teammates better, and 3) makes the game itself better by competing with honor.

3   Double-Goal Coaches are character educators who compete to win but never lose sight of the innumerable opportunities sports present to teach life lessons. Whether or not your child has a Double-Goal Coach, you, as a Second-Goal Parent, can encourage your athlete to aspire to be a Triple-Impact Competitor.

Understanding the High School Sports Landscape

The transition to high school can be jarring for teenagers. After having figured out a place for themselves in elementary and middle school, they now have to do it all over again, at what seems like much higher stakes.

The transition is also often a challenge for high school parents. Teenagers are changing rapidly and trying out new ways to relate to their parents as they move steadily and/or tentatively toward independence. And if your child is or aspires to be a high school athlete, there is a whole other set of challenges to negotiate.

What Parents Need to Know About High School Sports

PCA tapped its network of coaches, athletic directors, and parents to identify what high school sports parents need to know to help athletes thrive in high school sports. Here are four big ideas to help you understand your athlete's challenges and what you can do to help your teen thrive.

1) High school sports involves a *lot* of time and effort.

2) High school athletes are smack in the middle of a transition to adulthood.

3) High school sports programs have a chain of authority.

4) High school sports is a very public stage.

1) High School Sports Involves a *Lot* of Time and Effort

High school athletes are *busy!*

Balancing schoolwork, sports, friends, maybe a girlfriend or boyfriend, possibly a job all the while wondering about their future can frazzle even the most well-adjusted teen.

Sports alone can demand 12 to 20 hours per week for four months or more per sport. Imagine adding more than two workdays to your work schedule, and you will get the idea of what a high school sports commitment is like for a teen.

Plus, practicing is hard physical work. It takes a lot of energy – physical and emotional – to compete in sports, which can leave a teen athlete drained when she comes home.

What Can Parents Do?

Help your athlete plan and set priorities. Setting priorities and managing scarce time well is not something that comes naturally to most people. Help your teen develop these important life skills.

Before each sport season, sit down together to take a look at what is on his plate. Start first with academics (partly to signal how much you value learning). Help him map out the time he'll need to handle the demands of homework and sports so he'll have a better sense of how much time is available for other activities.

Encourage him to make two lists – a "to do list" and a "don't-do list." In setting priorities, saying no is often more important than saying yes.

Don't allow shortcuts in sleep and nutrition. Many high school athletes try to manage their heavy work load by sleeping less and eating on the run (usually junk food). Neither of these helps a student-athlete, especially those undergoing huge growth spurts. In fact, student-athletes need *more* sleep and *better* diets. Make sure your son or daughter has nutritious meals and snacks. And insist on them being in bed at a decent hour so they get the 9.25 hours of sleep they need according to the

National Sleep Foundation. Make sure your athlete understands that she will *perform better* if she eats and sleeps properly.

Encourage building in "down time." Just like muscles grow when they have rest between weight lifting sessions, your teen needs some down time to just chill, relax, do nothing, hang out, read for pleasure, or listen to music. Encourage him to build in time to do nothing.

Give your athlete a break. She will undoubtedly get tired and cranky at times. She may procrastinate. That's normal, so don't overreact and make a big problem out of what may be a transitory thing.

Don't panic if there is a crash. Sometimes, despite all preventive measures, the combination of athletics, academics, and extracurriculars overwhelm student-athletes, often in the middle of a season. Pulled between various pressures, teens can get stretched to a breaking point.

If this occurs, recognize that it's not unusual. Help your teen consider options for remedying it. Most often, improving time management, reassessing priorities, and self-advocacy is the answer. But sometimes, in extreme circumstances, your athlete may need to ask for greater flexibility from her coaches or teachers, who can allow a day off from practice or extend a deadline.

2)   High School Athletes Are Smack in the Middle of a Transition to Adulthood

Many parents forget from time to time that their teen is going through a big transition. Adolescence is a time of individuating, separation, and transition into adulthood. Developing independence is a natural process that should be nurtured, even though it can be difficult for parents who feel they are losing the little guy or gal that relied on them for so much.

Parents accustomed to coaching and managing the off-field affairs for the child's youth sports teams must now adjust to sitting in the stands and watching other people coach and run the athletic program. The parent is no longer in the driver's seat.

The good news is that sports is an ideal "practice arena" for teens to begin to flex their independence – and a great place for you to practice letting go. High school sports provides a chance to determine how seriously they want to pursue their sport(s), set their own goals and plan to achieve those goals, and learn to advocate appropriately for their own interests with their coaches and teammates.

Unfortunately, some parents lose sight of the importance of this transition, and sports instead becomes an unpleasant power struggle.

What Can Parents Do?

Encourage independence *and* the responsibility that goes with it. You do your teen no favors by micromanaging his affairs and making decisions for him. Instead, make him responsible for his athletic life. Allow him to choose what sports to play and the goals he wants to achieve. Give him greater responsibility for the accompanying logistics, be it washing uniforms, arranging rides, or fixing his own meals for trips.

Respect your athlete's choices. High school sports may present difficult choices for teens: Continue with a sport or quit? Specialize or play multiple sports? Play on the club team or high school team or both? Make the sacrifices necessary to earn a varsity letter or college scholarship? Listen to my coach or my dad? The answers to many of these questions go to the heart of a parent-child relationship.

Many parents invest so much time, effort, and money into their child's sports experience that they become heavily invested in these decisions. When a parent's sports aspirations conflict with those of their athlete, both parties can get hurt. As the adult, you may need to surrender your sport's dreams.

Help your athlete make her own educated decisions. This may require her to do research, list pros and cons, and talk with people she trusts. But, in the end, your teen will be better equipped for impending adulthood by making her own decisions.

Just listen. One of the greatest gifts you can give your athlete is to listen to her, especially when she is struggling. Managing a demanding schedule and increased responsibility can be daunting for high school athletes. And when they struggle, parents often aren't the first people they turn to for comfort – their peers are. Nonetheless, it's important for parents to "be there" for them.

Communicate unconditional support. High school is a time when teens are trying to prove themselves – to themselves, to their peer group, to the larger world. If they feel they also have to prove themselves to their parents, it will add unneeded pressure. Be explicit: "You don't have to be a great athlete or a great student because you are already a great person in my book." Repeat it throughout your teen's high school years. Whether she shows it or not, this will have a positive impact.

3. High School Sports Programs Have a Chain of Authority

Most high school sports' programs have a set chain of authority for resolving problems. Often the biggest problems in high school sports occur when parents circumvent the chain of authority, overstep their bounds to rectify a perceived problem or inequity (usually involving concerns about coaching strategy and/or their son or daughter's playing time), or poison the water by venting their concerns to other parents or athletes, including their own child.

To be sure, there may be times when teams under-perform, athletes are under-utilized by a coach, or the sports experience is less than ideal. These things happen, and that's unfortunate. But the larger issue is how you respond to your athlete's concerns – or your own concerns – in these situations. (Chapter 9 offers detailed advice on how to respond to specific problems.)

What can parents do?

Assume good will. Just like you, most coaches and athletic programs want what's best for your athlete.

Recognize who's in charge. This may be hard for you to accept, but you are not in charge of your child's high school sports experience. She is. Be supportive and helpful, but don't take over for her. Sports offers a great chance for your teen to learn responsibility. Don't waste the opportunity by taking over when there's a perceived problem.

Realize that coaches have to balance competing needs. Coaches must do what they think is best for a dozen or more players. On a team, the "pie" is limited and the coach cannot give every family everything it may want. Every player cannot play shortstop, quarterback, or point guard. The team concept requires give-and-take and mutual sacrifice for the sake of the whole.

Help your athlete learn to advocate for himself. If your teen complains about the coach, teammates, his playing time, or his role on the team, encourage him to think about how he wants to deal with it. Tell him you'll be happy to listen to him if he wants to talk about what he might do. You can even role-play how he might approach the coach, for example, if he wants to get more playing time.

Don't make derogatory comments about the coach to your teen or other parents or members of the team. Sadly, undermining coaches behind their backs is rampant in high school sports. This toxic behavior can devastate team culture, divide a team, and place high school athletes in an awkward middle between coach and parent. If you don't like the coach, keep it to yourself and don't poison the water.

If there's an issue you think may warrant intervening, proceed sensibly. There are some situations – physical or emotional abuse, for example – where you may decide you need to step in. (Note: Your child playing less than you would like is not a reason to intervene.) Here are some guidelines for intervening.

a. Don't intervene when you are angry or in emotional e-mails. Wait to cool down before you contact a coach or athletic director. Inflammatory e-mails do great damage. Assume that everything you write in an e-mail will be seen by exactly the people you don't want to see it.

b. Get all the information you can before you act. Don't assume you know what is going on, and don't assume your child's portrayal is the only or "true" one.

c. Consult with your athlete on your plans. Many athletes are horrified to learn that their parent intervened with a coach. It is crucial that you don't act in a way that undercuts or embarrasses your teen.

d. Act as if everyone is operating out of good will, even if you suspect they are not.

e. Figure out what success is before you act. Too often parents act out of emotion without knowing what they want to happen. Make sure you have an answer to the question, "What do you want to happen?" if you are asked.

f. Follow the chain of authority. Go to the coach first, even if you think he is the problem. You will ultimately get better results with the athletic director if you start with the coach. Similarly, the athletic director should always be contacted before an issue is brought to the principal or assistant principal.

4) High School Sports is a Very Public Stage

Athletes sometimes play in front of thousands of fans, and the press frequently covers high school sporting events. Colleges scout high schools for recruits. Athletes learn quickly that high school sports seem to matter more than youth sports.

Because of this public nature of high school sports, winning and "doing well" can become too important for athletes. The pressure to specialize, get private coaching, attend expensive camps, or purchase the best equipment becomes greater on athletes and parents at this level.

For athletes, this means that how they do on the field of play may result in extraordinary status rewards or awful public embarrassment (amplified by the experience of adolescence). It also means that adults – parents, coaches, and other community members – can get a little crazy from time to time and lose perspective.

Stress on student-athletes can push them to poor decisions. Athletes may be tempted to cheat or take shortcuts. They may lose sight of the fact that they are playing a game that should be fun rather than a high-stakes pressure cooker. Most seriously, steroid use and eating disorders are an unfortunate reality of high school athletics – a sign of the pressures kids are under. (See accompanying tables on Steroids and Eating Disorders on page 20.)

What can parents do?

Maintain a Second-Goal focus at all times. The scoreboard does matter, but not as much as the life lessons sports can teach. Keep your focus on life lessons, rather than measuring your teen's athletic success based on on-field performance. Knowing that someone loves and supports them no matter how they perform is huge, especially for developing teens.

Focus on your teen's effort rather than the outcome. Later in Chapter 5, I'll discuss the importance of encouraging a "growth mindset" with your athlete. For now, I'll just say that your expectations for your teen should be that she gives her best shot, not that she will succeed in everything.

Help your athlete keep sports in proper perspective. Adolescents can exaggerate the importance of success or failure. Encourage them to enjoy the moment and to periodically refocus on the big picture. In the final analysis, virtually all high school sports results will forgotten by everyone but those who participated.

Keep the lines of communication open. Let your teen vent about things that stress him out. It's not helpful for him to keep it bottled up. Make opportunities to be alone with your athlete – in the car, around the dinner table, on a hike – to listen to his feelings about his sports experiences.

Get professional help if needed. If you think your athlete may be using performance enhancing drugs or suffering from an eating disorder, it's better to be safe than sorry. Ask your doctor or friends for the name of a counselor who has helped others in your teen's situation.

Signs of Eating Disorders

- Preoccupation with weight or body
- Constant dieting, even when skinny
- Making excuses not to eat
- Going to the bathroom right after meals
- Taking diet pills or laxatives
- Eating in secret, at night, or alone
- Hoarding high calorie food
- Compulsive exercising
- Avoiding social settings that include food
- Obsession with food, calories, nutrition

Signs of Steroid Use

- Fast weight and muscle gains connected to a weight training program
- Aggressiveness, combative behavior
- Jaundice (yellow skin)
- Red or purple spots on the body
- Oily skin and severe acne breakouts
- Constant unpleasant breath
- Trembling
- Swelling of lower legs and feet

The Bright Side

This chapter paints a pretty stressful picture of what high school can be like for an athlete, but high school can be a glorious time of growth and change for a young person. It can be a time that he will remember fondly forever.

This is much more likely to happen if you understand your supporting role and play it to the hilt, which is exactly what I wish for you and your athlete.

Chapter 3 Take-Aways

1 High school sports involve a lot of time and effort. Athletes can become unduly stressed by social, academic, and athletic pressures. Parents can help by assisting in setting priorities, making sure kids get enough sleep and good nutrition, and encouraging down-time.

2 High school athletes are in the middle of a transition to adulthood. Sports provide an ideal "practice arena" for teens to practice independence and a great place for parents to practice letting go.

3 High school sports programs have a well-defined chain of authority. Parents create problems when they circumvent it when a concern or perceived inequity arises. Parents are best served to help athletes advocate for themselves.

4 High school sports is a very public stage. The pressure to win on the scoreboard can bring out the worst in coaches, parents, and athletes. Parents can help by maintaining a Second-Goal focus on the life lessons sports offer and encouraging effort over results.

CHAPTER FOUR

First Things First: Getting Straight with Goals

"My dad coached all of my youth soccer teams while I was growing up, and we were always fighting over what had happened during the game that day, or how I wasn't working hard enough in practice...Then my dad took the Positive Coaching Alliance classes. Since then, he has definitely eased up, and it is much easier for both of us to take advice from each other and understand where the other person is coming from. Since PCA, my dad and I get along so much better, on and off the field."

Christina, Division I College Athlete

In the course of speaking to thousands of sports parents all across the United States, I've noticed the sharp tension that often exists between parent and athlete. What should be a wonderful shared experience too often becomes a source of conflict between parent and child. Christina's experience is far from unusual.

This is too bad because a family's experience with high school sports has the potential to enhance the relationship between parent and teen – long after the days on the playing field have ended.

The place where parent-athlete relationships usually start to go wrong is with goals. Parents often don't take the time to explicitly examine their own goals for their athlete in sports or ensure that their behavior is consistent with their identified goals.

Nor do they consider that their goals may not match their son or daughter's goals. So much tension occurs when a parent's dreams conflict with the ideas of their increasingly independent teen, who may have a very different conception of how he wants his life to play out.

The 100-Points Exercise

We start PCA parent workshops with an exercise that gets right to the heart of this issue. I encourage you to take the time to fill out this form right now. I am confident you won't be sorry.

You have 100 "points" that you can divide across the goals on the form (or a separate piece of paper) in any way you want. You can even write in your own goals if the form doesn't have all the ones that are important to you. Remember to fill out the form in terms of what your goals for your son or daughter in sports are (later we'll address your teen's goals). Your points should add up to 100, more or less – no one's watching!

What are YOUR goals for your teen in high school sports?
_____ Become a good athlete
_____ Learn to play the sport
_____ Learn teamwork as part of a team
_____ Win
_____ Gain increased self-confidence
_____ Learn to deal with defeat
_____ Physical fitness
_____ Learn "life lessons"
_____ Have fun
_____ Make friends
_____ Earn a varsity letter
_____ Earn a college scholarship
_____ Other (specify:_____)
_____ Other (specify:_____)
__100__ TOTAL

What Parents Say

In hundreds of workshops, we have learned that most parents have similar hopes and goals for their athletes. Parents often give significant points to physical fitness, having fun, making friends, increased self-confidence, and learning life lessons.

A father once gave all 100 points to having fun because he said that all the other benefits become possible if his son sticks with sports. And if he is having fun, he'll keep coming back. If it stops being fun, he won't continue and the many benefits listed here will be lost.

Many parents resonate with the goal of learning to deal with defeat without becoming defeated. I've heard moving testimonials of parents rebounding from failure in their jobs to ultimately experience success. People nod their heads when I note that it's hard to learn how to bounce back from defeat if you don't experience defeat.

Rarely do parents in PCA workshops give many points to winning. Sitting in the low-key atmosphere of a classroom or school cafeteria, winning just doesn't get much value or respect.

How Parents Act

Then comes the moment of revelation. We say to the parents, "You've given the vast majority of your points to these wonderful benefits of playing sports. But what happens to this list when you go to a sports competition? All but one of these items goes out the window. Which one seems to get all 100 points if we look at the way parents act on the sidelines?"

This often leads to sheepish expressions because we all have acted in conflict with our highest goals and made *winning* the be-all and end-all of sports.

Your 100 Points

Let's look at your 100 points. Are there any surprises? Any areas where you need to work to bring your sideline behavior in line with your goals?

Your Teen's 100 Points

I recommend you ask your teen to fill out the version of this form on page 68. Then sit down with her to discuss her goals, which may produce some "aha moments."

Ask why she distributed her points the way she did. Try not to say too much at this point – you want to get her talking about her goals. Ask open-ended questions such as, "I notice you have 50 points on 'Fun.' Why did you put the most points on that?" Then really listen.

Later you can extend the conversation by sharing your goal sheet with your teen. Talk about why the two of you gave different amounts of points to various items. Many parents have told us that this has led to great sharing and some valuable insights about their athlete.

When Goals Differ

You may find that your goals are very different from your child's goals, a realization which can save both of you a lot of unnecessary suffering because so much conflict can stem from a simple misunderstanding about what another person's goals are.

Research shows that the majority of high school athletes want to partici-pate, have fun, be with friends, and play sports at a more competent level. Sometimes parents want something quite different – headlines, awards, college scholarships, or a shot at professional athletics. Sometimes they want these things without even consciously being aware that these are their goals.

Imposing your goals on your athlete is a recipe for disaster. Knowing how what your teen wants differs from what you want – and respecting that difference – is an important step in maintaining a clear channel of communication between parent and child that can strengthen your relationship through whatever stresses arise during the high school years.

Athletic directors and coaches tell us that the most difficult and challenging parents are often those with the greatest sports ambitions, such as wanting their athlete to earn a college scholarship. "First-Goal" Parents who focus solely on their child's on-field achievements are more likely to break rules, undermine team culture, or take unethical or mean-spirited actions to get their way.

This is unfortunate because only a very small percentage of high school athletes earn college scholarships. Parents who obsess about playing time or how many points their child scored frequently miss the opportunity to reinforce life lessons through sports. Their athlete, scholarship in hand or not, is the worse for that.

And – although this may not be obvious at first – if your teen does have the potential to earn a college scholarship, your behaving as a Second-Goal Parent will give your athlete the best chance to excel, as you'll see as you read the rest of this book.

Get straight with goals, and keep the Second Goal in the forefront of your parenting. You, your athlete, coaches, and teammates will all be the better for it.

Chapter 4 Take-Aways

1 Make sure you are clear on your goals for your teen in sports. Use the 100-Point Exercise to help clarify them.

2 Let your son or daughter do the 100-Point Exercise, and then have a discussion about your respective goals. Listen more than talk.

3 Imposing your goals in sports on your teen is a recipe for disaster. Knowing what your teen wants in sports – and respecting the difference if her wants are different than yours – is key to maintaining a healthy relationship.

CHAPTER FIVE

Avoiding the Talent Trap

At one time or another, most sports parents will fantasize about their child's success on the playing field – throwing the winning touchdown or swishing the game-winning basket at the buzzer. Long before an athlete performs for his high school team, a parent might wonder, "Could my child have the talent to win a college scholarship?"

These feelings and aspirations are natural for parents, but here's the reality: the chances of any child "earning" a college scholarship are not good. NCAA statistics indicate that only 6.1 percent of high school senior baseball players play baseball in college. For football, it's 5.7 percent. For basketball, it's 3.0 percent for boys and 3.3 percent for girls.

These are long odds to even play in college, but the number of athletes getting athletic scholarships is much smaller. About 2.3 percent of college athletes receive a scholarship. And realize that only about 20 percent of scholarship athletes receive a full ride. The vast majority of college scholarship athletes receive partial scholarships that may be just a sliver of the entire cost of college.

Reality for Scholarship Athletes

I intentionally used the term "earn" a scholarship in the above section because college athletes work hard. They spend many hours in season on their sport. Their practice schedule determines which courses they can (and can't) take, and games mean missing classes, making up exams, and trying to study on buses and in hotel rooms.

Off-season doesn't necessarily mean a break from their sport. As one famous saying has it, "The season is where teams become great. Off-season is where athletes become great." Many college programs have "voluntary" workouts that athletes often feel they dare not miss without jeopardizing their playing time the following season.

College athletes pay a price for their scholarships that students who are awarded academic scholarships do not. Academic scholarships typically do not require anything other than studying and learning – what college is, after all, all about.

Now I know many former college athletes who regret not a single moment of their college sports experience. I also know some who feel they "missed" the complete college experience and wonder if they made the right decision.

My point is not that college scholarships are not worth the effort. Rather, they involve a cost as well as a benefit, even if your child is one of the few who is awarded one.

Setting a goal of your teen winning an athletic scholarship is seldom a winning hand. As we've seen in Chapter 4, there are so many other advantages to participating in sports that have nothing to do with earning a scholarship.

And focusing on your teen's talent can also lead you to devalue his current experience while you dream about what he might be able to do at the next level. If you are just starting the high school journey with your teen, you may find it hard to believe how quickly time will fly during the high school years. But trust me – before you know it, it will be over. Rather than seeing high school sports as a ticket to a higher place, seeing it as valuable in its own right can help you be present in the moment to enjoy it.

But there is a much more important reason to avoid focusing on talent – it can actually harm your teen's ability to succeed, in sports and life.

The Growth Mindset

Focusing on talent can be a trap.

Carol Dweck of Stanford University, author of *Mindset: The New Psychology of Success,* has identified two different mindsets that possess enormous implications for sports parents.

The first is the "fixed mindset," in which one sees one's ability as set. Either you are talented athletically or you aren't. Either you are smart or you aren't. This mindset is a dead-end because whether you succeed or not is determined by something totally outside your control.

The other is the "growth mindset." You believe in your ability to grow and improve, regardless of where you start. This is a wonderful thought for any young person: "I can get smarter (or better at learning a foreign language or excelling in a sport or…) if I work hard at it."

If your teen does something well, either on the playing field or in the classroom, Dweck's research offers clear guidance on how to respond.

For example, you might say, "Wow, that was a great play. You are really good!" This focus on talent reinforces a fixed mindset and the idea that your son or daughter has little or no control over his development. A tough challenge in the future then becomes even tougher because talent-ed people aren't supposed to be stumped by a challenge.

On the other hand, you could say, "Wow, that was a great play. You've really been working hard, and it's paying off." This reinforces a growth mindset that her good play is a result of her effort, which will more likely cause her to try harder in the future when faced with a challenge that stymies her initially.

It's All About Effort

Whenever you can, stress to your teen how important effort is in helping people improve and learn. Avoid attributing any success your son or daughter has to his talent (or intelligence, for that matter) to avoid the talent trap. You can use "You're-the-Kind-of-Person-Who" statements to reinforce the growth mindset in times of failure and success:

■ **Failure:** "I know you must be disappointed (that you missed a key shot, or that you didn't get selected for the lead role in the play), but one of the things I admire about you is that *you're the kind of person who* bounces back and keeps trying until you succeed."

■ **Success:** "I was excited to see you play so well. I think you're getting better because *you're the kind of person who* works hard at something until you improve."

Talent and Entitlement

As we've seen, focusing on talent rather than effort endangers a person's ability to thrive under future challenges. But there is another way in which a focus on talent harms athletes and their families.

Ingrained in our sports culture is the notion that talent entails privileges. At an early age, the athlete who shows signs of talent is often told, explicitly and implicitly, that he is special. Talented athletes often get passes with regards to schoolwork. They can be catered to by coaches who see them as a ticket to a winning season or even to a better coaching position.

The key message: you don't have to work as hard as less talented athletes. This is a horrendous disservice to athletes. The talented athlete with a poor work ethic will soon enough run into competitors who combine talent with hard work, and the result will not be pretty. Professional sports is littered with examples of supremely talented individuals who underperformed because they never got used to working hard.

For the high school athlete, the talent entitlement attitude can poison the entire high school sports experience. Parents obsessed with an often-inflated sense of their child's talent can create conflict over playing time, academic requirements, and other things that can wreak havoc on teams, programs, and kids.

The antidote to all this is the powerful idea that talent brings with it responsibility rather than privilege. A wonderful mantra for parents to reinforce with their talented child is "To whom much (talent) is given, much (effort) is required."

Notice that this works regardless of how talented your child actually will turn out to be. If she has the natural ability to go on to excel in sports at higher levels, a strong work ethic will help. If she doesn't, it will serve her well in whatever she decides to do with her life.

Effort and Transformation

The teen years are a time of transformation. The person entering high school and the graduate of the same name and DNA are very different people. Vast changes – in physical size and capability, emotional maturity, and interests – occur from age 14 to 18. As parents we sometimes get locked into a view of our child without realizing that our teen is a work in progress.

An early-maturing athlete entering high school with big hopes to be a starter or even a star may find that late bloomers experience growth spurts that leave him on the bench much of the time. Another teen may go from the back of the pack to the front as she develops mental toughness and superior physical conditioning. The kid who was batty about baseball may decide he wants to put his effort and energy behind an entirely different, non-sports activity.

The high school experience can be a roller coaster for both teen and parent. Keeping in mind the importance of a growth mindset and fostering it in your child can help smooth out the bumps.

A youth who embraces the growth mindset will be able to apply that to whatever activity she undertakes. A study by K. A. Ericsson concluded that it takes an individual 10 years and 10,000 hours of deliberate practice to become an elite athlete. It is the rare individual who is willing to put that much effort into an activity for that long without enjoying the process, which brings me to an important final point on effort.

Effort and Enjoyment Entwined

So far this chapter has been all about how effort and hard work are keys to success, which is true. But what also needs to be said is that effort can be immensely enjoyable. When we work hard on something, especially something that we really care about, it is enjoyable!

When I look back on my life, the times I remember most vividly and fondly are those when I worked really hard to accomplish something. Effort is not the opposite of enjoyment. The two are entwined in a wonderful way.

I also think that a growth mindset engenders joy at working hard. When we believe that we can achieve something if we just keep working at it, it makes the process of working hard more fun.

I encourage you to help your athlete understand this connection between effort and enjoyment. You might even ask a leading question such as, "You really were working your tail off tonight. And you know what? It looked like you were enjoying yourself at the same time. Is that right?" You might also talk appreciatively about the times you have worked hard and how much you enjoyed it.

Chapter 5 Take-Aways

1 Focusing on a teen's athletic talent rather than effort is a trap that can actually harm her ability to reach her potential. Focusing on talent also breeds an attitude of entitlement that is a disservice to athletes.

2 Foster a "growth mindset" in your teen, with a focus on effort and improvement. This will help him recognize that success in sports and other activities depends more on how hard he works than on his talent.

3 Help your teen understand that effort and hard work is usually entwined with enjoyment and is a wonderful gift that will serve her well for the rest of her life.

CHAPTER SIX

The ELM Tree of Mastery

The next three chapters introduce material crucial for any athlete who desires to become a Triple-Impact Competitor. Chapter 7 discusses the Emotional Tank, a key to Level 2 of the Triple-Impact Competitor: making teammates better.

Chapter 8 describes Honoring the Game, a Level 3 concept which guides how Triple-Impact Competitors compete to make the game itself better.

Let's start with the ELM Tree of Mastery, which is integral to Level 1 of Triple-Impact Competitor: making oneself better.

The Pony in the Sport Psychology Lecture

I remember sitting in a sport psychology lecture about 10 years ago trying desperately to make sense of the tables of tiny numbers on the screen behind the speaker. Reminded of an old joke about an optimistic boy surrounded by horse manure, I kept thinking, "There must be a pony in here somewhere."

I took pages of notes but couldn't quite figure out the "so-what factor" for coaches and sports parents. This troubled me because I had just launched Positive Coaching Alliance, and I felt obligated to translate the powerful insights of sport psychology into practical tools that millions of coaches and sports parents – the vast majority of whom have no access to a sport psychology consultant – could use to get the best out of athletes.

A few days later while on a long run it hit me. The key principle of sport psychology that was underpinning the complex lecture is that you get the best results when you focus on what you can control and block out the rest.

That's it. That is the secret of sport psychology: focus on what you can control and block out the rest.

Now this is a big idea, with implications far beyond the playing field. But what is controllable and what isn't in the lives of athletes? The biggest uncontrollable is the scoreboard outcome of a competition. You can't control who wins a game: the quality of your opposition, officials' calls, the weather, and injuries all affect the outcome. The list of uncontrollables is endless.

Then what are the crucial aspects of competition that you *can* control?

That question led to a formulation that has been a central idea of Positive Coaching Alliance ever since, the ELM Tree of Mastery, which closely aligns with the Growth Mindset described in Chapter 5.

The ELM Tree of Mastery

The ELM Tree of Mastery is

E for Effort,
L for Learning and improvement, and
M for Mistakes, how we respond to mistakes and the fear of them.

What was buried in the initially mystifying sport psychology lecture were the three keys to success in sports (and life, for that matter).

Your teen absolutely will be successful sooner or later if she

- routinely gives her best effort
- has a "teachable spirit" and learns from everything that happens to her
- doesn't let mistakes (or fear of mistakes) stop her

Triple-Impact Competitors Redefine "Winner"

Whereas the larger culture is obsessed with results on the scoreboard, the ELM Tree focuses on how hard you work.

Implicit in the ELM Tree is that comparisons with others are not helpful. The person you want to compare yourself to is you. Are you better than you were two weeks ago? Will you be better at the end of the season than you are now? If so, you will be a winner, regardless of the temporary results on the scoreboard.

Emphasizing the ELM Tree of Mastery, and not results on the scoreboard, is what I call redefining "winning." Let's compare the "scoreboard" definition of a winner with the "mastery" definition.

Scoreboard Definition	Mastery Definition
Results	Effort
Comparison with others	Learning and improvement
Mistakes are not okay	Mistakes are okay

Triple-Impact Competitors focus on mastery as a way to become the best they can be. They achieve success on the scoreboard, as we will learn later in this chapter, as a by-product of their relentless pursuit of mastery.

The Power (and Paradox) of the ELM Tree

There is a lot of research and supporting material behind the ELM Tree of Mastery, but let me put it simply.

1) **ELM = Control:** Athletes can't control the outcome of a competition. But they absolutely can learn to control all elements of the ELM Tree: a) their level of effort, b) whether they learn from their experience, and c) how they respond to the inevitable mistakes they will make. Internalizing the ELM Tree makes athletes feel more in control of their own destiny.

2) **Anxiety:** When athletes feel in control, their anxiety decreases. Decreased anxiety frees up nervous energy so it can be focused on accomplishing a task rather than worrying about failing.

3) **Self-Confidence:** Self-confidence also increases when athletes feel in control. And when self-confidence increases, athletes tend to work harder and stick to it longer as research by Stanford's Albert Bandura has demonstrated. This is a *huge* idea so I am going to repeat it: if you increase a teen's self-confidence, he will work harder and stick to a task longer without giving up.

That's the power of the ELM Tree. The paradox is that by focusing on mastery, athletes actually do better on the scoreboard. You win more by not focusing on winning!

Research bears this out. During the 2000 Summer Olympics, sports psychologist Joan Duda of the University of Birmingham, England, conducted research on athletes coached in a mastery environment and those coached in a traditional "scoreboard" environment with a primary emphasis on bottom-line results. She discovered a statistically significant difference in performance – athletes coached to focus on mastery won significantly more medals than their counterparts whose focus was on winning medals.

Athletes are more likely to internalize the ELM Tree if they have coaches and parents who emphasize the virtues of mastery and de-emphasize results on the scoreboard. This, in turn, helps them feel in control, experience decreased anxiety, and feel more self-confident, so they can perform better.

Here's how you can provide this advantage for your athlete.

The ELM Tree Needs Constant Watering

It is not enough to just tell your son or daughter about the ELM Tree of Mastery. The culture of professional sports is not about the ELM Tree. Rather, the dominant sports culture constantly undermines a mastery approach by focusing almost exclusively on scoreboard winners, ignoring great efforts that come up short, showing disdain for those who don't win, and showing and telling in so many ways that the only thing ultimately that matters is winning on the scoreboard.

It is not surprising in light of the 24/7 media saturation in professional sports that it is hard for a mastery approach in high school sports to take hold. That's where you come in.

The ELM Tree requires constant watering. Introduce the ELM Tree to your son or daughter and talk about it often, ideally as part of becoming a Triple-Impact Competitor.

- Before a game: "I know it's a big game and you may feel pressure to win. But just remember to have fun and give it your all out on the field – that's all you can really control."

- After a game: "I really liked the way you competed today. You worked so hard and you didn't let any of your mistakes sidetrack you."

The more you use the ELM Tree concept with your son or daughter, the more it will be able to help her focus on what is important.

The Mistake Ritual

No successful person is successful in everything. Many successful people credit their success to being willing to risk making a mistake and learn from it. Chris Larsen, the co-founder of E-Loan, tells of sitting in Jim Collins' entrepreneurship class at the Stanford Graduate School of Business. Collins told the MBA students they were too risk averse. They could afford to fail a few times, learn from their mistakes, and then go on to succeed. The phrase that Chris remembers was, "Cut the lifeboats." Chris says that he likely would never have started a new company like E-Loan if he hadn't heard Collins' comment about the lifeboats and not fearing mistakes.

Mistakes are what kids worry about the most. The fear of making a mistake occupies so much mindshare of high school athletes that it can paralyze them. Consider the typical reaction from the stands that an athlete hears or sees after making a glaring mistake – many parents groan, slap their head, frown, or yell corrective instructions.

If we can reduce the fear of making a mistake, there will be much more energy available to learn the game and excel at it.

At PCA we've developed the "mistake ritual." A mistake ritual is simply a gesture and/or statement that individuals use to ward off the fear of making mistakes so they don't play timidly. A mistake ritual allows you to quickly "reset" and get ready for the next play or decision without wallowing in the past and beating yourself up for having made a mistake.

There are many mistake rituals, but here are two that we especially like. One is "Flushing Mistakes." When your teen makes a mistake on the playing field, you can simply make a motion like you are flushing a toilet. You can add commentary to the flush: "It's okay, Omar. Flush it. Next play."

Another mistake ritual is "No Sweat." This involves swiping two fingers across one's forehead like you were flicking sweat from your brow. "No sweat. Forget it and have fun!"

Chapter 6 Take-Aways

1 Talk with your teen about the ELM Tree of Mastery to help her be successful in sports and life. The acronym "ELM" reminds her to always give her best effort, to have a "teachable spirit" and learn from her experiences, and to not let mistakes (or fear of mistakes) stop her. Because the dominant sports culture undermines a mastery approach, water the ELM Tree frequently so she internalizes it as her own and is able to apply it to challenges she faces in sports and life.

2 The ELM Tree of Mastery works because it focuses your teen on what she can control, which decreases anxiety and improves self-confidence. This improves overall performance in any aspect of life.

3 Use a Mistake Ritual to help your teen learn to not fear mistakes and to bounce back quickly from them.

Your Athlete's Emotional Tank

Have you ever stumbled onto something so basic and powerful that it changes the way you see almost everything?

For years I wondered why I could feel great about a talk I gave on Thursday night and feel terrible about the same talk to a similar group on Saturday morning. Then I read about the "Emotional Tank" in Ross Campbell's wonderful book, *How to Really Love Your Child*. Each of us has an Emotional Tank like the gas tank in a car. If our tank is empty, we can't expect to drive across the country. If our tank is full, we can go a long way.

On Thursday, people in the audience filled my Emotional Tank. They nodded their head when I spoke. They smiled and laughed at my jokes. They asked questions indicating they were engaged with my ideas. Some even thanked me afterwards for an insight they believed might help them be a better coach or parent.

On Saturday morning, no one did anything to fill my Emotional Tank. They scowled, nodded off, talked to each other when I was talking. They drained my Emotional Tank.

No wonder I felt like a gift to the audience on Thursday night and a fraud on Saturday morning. And it all revolved around what was happening to a tank I didn't even know I had.

The Portable Home Team Advantage

Athletes do better when their Emotional Tanks are full. We all could use a "portable home team advantage" in our lives. Unconditional support and genuine praise encourages us and improves performance and attitude.

An athlete with a drained Emotional Tank likely will not perform as well as that same athlete with an overflowing Emotional Tank. That's partly why the home team wins almost 60 percent of the time in college and professional sports.

Athletes with full Emotional Tanks are more coachable. They are more open to coaches' suggestions. When Emotional Tanks are full, people tend to be optimistic, deal better with adversity, and are more capable of changing their behavior in response to feedback given to them, even by their parents!

When Emotional Tanks are low, people tend to be pessimistic, give up more easily, and become defensive in the face of criticism.

Filling and Draining Your Teen's Emotional Tank

The Emotional Tank is a powerful idea, but it is not rocket science. You can fill your teen's tank in these ways:

Tank Fillers	Examples
Truthful, specific praise	· "Nice effort! You hustled and fought for four quarters." · "An 'A' on your math test! I noticed you studied hard to prepare for the test."
Express appreciation	· "It was great the way you pumped up your teammates before the team made its comeback." · "Thanks for helping out with your little sister."
Listening	· "What else did you like about the game?" · "What did you think of the election?"
Nonverbal actions	· Smiling, clapping, nodding, thumbs up

Praise can be a tank-filler, but it needs to be truthful and specific. It's fine to say "Good job." But it is so much more powerful to say, "I really appreciated the way you took so much care with this project. Your hard work and attention to detail made this a big success."

Be careful not to heap praise when it isn't warranted. Teens are very discerning about what's real and what's disingenuous, especially with parents.

Listening is one of the most powerful tank fillers, especially when parents really listen. Adopt a tell-me-more-attitude to understand what's going on for your teen and to foster healthy dialogue.

While we all need refreshers in tank filling, most of us are pretty natural tank drainers. We often find it easier to see what is wrong and comment on it than to reinforce laudable behavior. Here are common tank drainers:

Tank Drainers	Examples
Criticize and correct	· "You could have gotten more loose balls. Be more aggressive, like Maria." · "That grade isn't good enough. Next time it better be an A."
Sarcasm	· "What were you thinking on that play?" · "Will you ever clean your room?"
Ignoring	· "Not now." · "Maybe later."
Nonverbal	· Frowning, eye-rolling, heavy sighing

The Magic Ratio

Research has shown that the optimal ratio of tank-fillers to criticisms is 5 to 1. Professor John Gottman at the University of Washington calls this the Magic Ratio. I love that name because you really do see some magical things happen as you get close to a 5:1 ratio of positives to criticisms.

In Gottman's work with married couples, he found that couples at the 5:1 level tended to stay married, while at lower ratios divorces were more likely. Research in the classroom also indicates a 5:1 ratio is ideal to stimulate children's learning.

You might consider keeping track of your "plus/minus" ratio for a while to see what your baseline is. Then work to get it up to the Magic level and enjoy the results.

Criticism Transformed

Although criticism tends to drain people's tanks, it is not a bad thing. Criticism can help all of us grow and improve. But the catch is we have to be open to hearing and considering the criticism. And that is where the Emotional Tank transforms criticism into "receivable feedback."

Part of being a parent is having hard conversations with our kids when necessary. And being a consistent tank-filler doesn't mean you will never have to have a hard conversation with your son or daughter. But it does mean that your teen will be more likely to change in response to that hard conversation.

Here are some proven ways of making it more likely that your athlete will hear you and consider your feedback.

a) **Avoid Non-Teachable Moments:** There are some moments when it's harder for people to hear and receive criticism. Right after your athlete strikes out with the bases loaded is not a good time to discuss the benefits of resiliency. There's just too much emotional turmoil. Wait out non-teachable moments and keep your powder dry for later.

b) **Criticize in Private:** It's easier to hear criticism in private than in front of others where it is easy to feel embarrassed and become defensive. Respect your teen's need for dignity by talking to her privately.

c) **Ask Permission:** Sometimes you can short-circuit defensiveness by "asking permission." "Emily, I noticed something about the way you were dealing with a teammate that concerned me. Are you open to hearing it?" If Emily says yes, she is more likely to consider your comment. If she says no, you create great curiosity in her by saying, "Okay, no problem. Let me know if you change your mind." If you come back with the same question later, she is likely to say yes.

d) If-Then Statements: People are more likely to take criticism if they feel in control. If-Then Statements do this. "If you get your homework done tonight, then you'll be able to sleep in later in the morning."

e) Criticism Sandwich: By sandwiching your criticism between two positive statements, you make it more likely that it will be heard.

Triple-Impact Competitors Are Tank-Fillers

So far I've focused on you filling your child's Emotional Tank. But Triple-Impact Competitors are themselves tank fillers. Level 2 of the Triple-Impact Competitor model is about making teammates better, and a principal way Triple-Impact Competitors do that is by filling the E-Tanks of their teammates.

You can start to help your athlete become a proficient E-Tank Filler by talking about your own experience with it. If you had a tough day at work, when you get home you can say, "Boy, I had a tough day today. I felt like my E-Tank was being drained all day long." If your teen expresses appreciation for something you have done, you can say, "Thank you! That really fills my E-Tank."

You can also use a process we call "narrated modeling" to make sure that people don't misinterpret or even miss completely what you are doing. Simply share your process with your athlete. "My colleague at work was pretty down today, so I went out of my way to find something I could tell her to fill her tank. And I think it helped because she was much more positive and energetic the rest of the day."

Talking about filling E-Tanks and modeling tank-filling behavior in the home can be a powerful determiner of whether your teen becomes a tank-filler. And people who fill Emotional Tanks are likely to be successful in whatever they do in life.

Sometimes You Have to Fill Your Own Tank

The world is often unforgiving. Your teen may one day have to perform in an environment where no one will fill her Emotional Tank. Some people believe that the way to prepare young people for "the real world" is to get them used to nasty behavior (e.g., via a nasty, snarly coach) so they will be used to it when they encounter it in the larger world.

I reject this idea. I am convinced that people who grow up having their Emotional Tanks filled on a regular basis are going to be more able to deal effectively with bullies or other tank drainers they cannot avoid (such as an abusive boss). For one thing, they may not be as willing to submit to demeaning behavior as people who have been beaten down by long-term tank-draining behavior. They also are less likely to blame themselves for a supervisor's abusive behavior. They are more likely to say, "My boss is a jerk, but I don't need to let it get to me. I'm going to continue doing my job until I can find a better one."

Chapter 7 Take-Aways

1 An Emotional Tank is like a car's gas tank. People with full Emotional Tanks (from praise, thanks, and non-verbal positives) are more optimistic, better able to deal with adversity, and more open to feedback. When Emotional Tanks are drained (with insensitive criticism, sarcasm, and non-verbal downers), people are more pessimistic, give up more easily, and become defensive in the face of criticism. Triple-Impact Competitors look for ways to fill teammates' Emotional Tanks.

2 Strive to reach the Magic Ratio. Research has shown that the optimal ratio of tank-fillers to criticisms is 5 to 1. Also, use the Magic Ratio with other adults involved in sports, like coaches and officials.

3 Provide constructive criticism to your teen using techniques that take into account when and how to deliver criticism so your athlete can hear it and be more likely to act upon it.

Honoring the Game: Sportsmanship Reconsidered

Each year Positive Coaching Alliance compiles a list of the best and worst sports moments of the year. Not surprisingly, the media usually focuses on the Bottom 10 list and ignores the Top 10 list. Often the perpetrators are sports parents:

- A soccer mom, upset with her daughter's performance, pulled over and left her on the side of the freeway after a tournament.

- A softball dad brought a gun to practice to intimidate his daughter's coach because he wasn't giving his daughter enough playing time.

- A wrestling dad rushed out on the mat to body slam his son's opponent because he believed the other boy was cheating.

While we can tut-tut about the individual behavior of the parents who made the Bottom 10 List, the real problem is one of organizational culture.

A Crucial Mistake

At Positive Coaching Alliance, we define culture as "the way we do things here." The underlying problem is that high school sports has adopted the professional sports way of doing things.

As we discussed in Chapter 2, professional sports is an entertainment business with the goal all businesses have of making a profit. This requires entertaining fans, which in turn usually requires a winning team. Thus at the professional level, a win-at-all-cost mentality too often prevails. And because winning seems so important, pro sports fans tend to see their role as doing whatever they can to help "their" team win.

Because high school sports resembles professional sports – in rules, equipment, strategy – many people make the crucial mistake of thinking the two are the same. But pro sports and high school sports are fundamentally different enterprises. High school is about developing young men and women into great people who contribute to their community and achieve success in their careers and family lives.

That means that sports parents need to behave in a completely different way from pro sports fans – behavior we call "Honoring the Game."

The ROOTS of Honoring the Game

Honoring the Game, the central idea of Level 3 of being a Triple-Impact Competitor, is a more robust version of sportsmanship. Unfortunately, sportsmanship has lost much of its power to inspire and now seems like a list of don't-do's, like "Don't yell at officials" or "Don't throw your helmet." Honoring the Game is a concept to inspire and motivate people to live up to their best, rather than simply to be restricted from acting down to their worst.

If we want family members who help each other achieve their dreams, neighbors who are friendly and pitch in, business owners who pursue profit ethically, people from different traditions and backgrounds who respect one another – in short, if we want everyday decency in our society – then we can begin by teaching our teens how to compete in sports with grace and humility.

The ROOTS of Honoring the Game describe the behavior we want to teach and model, where ROOTS represents respect for: **R**ules, **O**pponents, **O**fficials, **T**eammates, and **S**elf.

Rules: We want to win the way the game is supposed to be played. We refuse to bend the rules even when we can get away with it, whether anyone is looking or not. Rules have been developed and carefully modified to make games as fair as possible. Breaking them undercuts fairness.

No rulebook can cover every situation. There will always be ambiguity that the rules simply don't address. Crafty individuals can find ways to circumvent the exact wording of any rule. People who Honor the Game respect both the spirit and the letter of the rules.

Opponents: A worthy opponent is a gift.

Imagine a tug-of-war with no one at the other end of the rope. Without opponents, competitive sports make no sense. It's not much fun to beat up on a much weaker opponent (or be tromped by a much stronger one). We are challenged when we have a worthy opponent, one who brings out our best. Just think about how the level of play is elevated when evenly matched rivals compete against each other.

"Fierce and friendly" says it all. You try as hard as you can to win. If you knock down an opponent going for the ball, you grab the loose ball and try to score. But when the whistle blows, you help your opponent up. Sports give the chance to get to know athletes you compete against, even become friends with them, without ever letting up when the game is on.

Officials: Officials are integral as guides to fairness in the game. Honoring the Game means you respect officials even when you disagree, even when they are wrong. There is never an excuse for treating officials with disrespect. No matter what.

Teammates: Never do anything, on or off the field, to embarrass your teammates. Honoring the Game involves behaving in a way that one's teammates and family would be proud of.

Self: The foundation of Honoring the Game is respect for oneself. Individuals with self-respect would never dishonor the game because they have their own standards that they want to live up to. Always.

I'm often asked if I expect people to Honor the Game when their opponents don't. That's what having your own standards means. Triple-Impact Competitors don't lower their standards because someone else does, even an opponent who gains an advantage. If you win by dishonoring the game, of what value is the victory?

Model Honoring the Game

Your actions, more than anything else, will teach your athlete about Honoring the Game. As you share in your teen's sports experience:

■ Talk about opponents respectfully, and never demonize them as "the enemy."

■ Cheer good plays by both teams. One father set the goal for himself that someone who doesn't already know which team his daughter played on wouldn't be able to tell from his sideline behavior.

■ Demonstrate respect for officials by not responding to missed calls. You can also point out bad calls made that benefit your athlete's team. "He missed that one in our favor. I guess the calls are going both ways today."

■ If you have access to them, thank and shake hands with the officials after the game. And encourage your athlete do so as well. As those of us who have tried it know, officials have the most difficult – and thankless – job in sports. Most high school sports officials are paid modestly for their efforts and are subject to abuse from adults on the sidelines. They deserve our gratitude and respect.

Seize Teachable Moments

With the ROOTS of Honoring the Game as a framework, high school sports provide an endless procession of teachable moments. Seize those moments to talk with your athlete about Honoring the Game in the context of your wanting him to be a Triple-Impact Competitor.

Whenever a member of your athlete's or the opposing team does something that Honors the Game (or not), you can use it as grist for a conversation. "Did you think what that player did was Honoring the Game? Why or why not?" Likewise, watching sporting events with your teen presents countless teachable moments.

The S in ROOTS especially provides an opportunity for powerful conversations with your teen about commitment to a set of values.

You might say: "You said you wanted to be a Triple-Impact Competitor, right? How can Honoring the Game help with that? And how can Honoring the Game now, as an athlete, make you a better person in the long run?"

Develop a Self-Control Routine

If you are the kind of person who gets upset at games, develop a self-control routine you can use when something happens that might trigger your temper, such as an official making a bad call or an opposing player doing something disrespectful. Imagine things that hit your hot buttons and see yourself remaining calm.

Count backward from 20, turn away from the game to take several deep breaths, or talk to yourself. ("I can do this. I can model respectful behavior for my child.") One mother's self-control routine involved exercise. Rather than watch from the sideline, she walked around the field before the game to ensure there wasn't anything that might trip her up. Then during the game she continuously circled the field. She improved her fitness while keeping up with the game at a distance that left the game in the hands of the players.

Be aware of your tendencies. We've all seen childish or reprehensible behavior in the stands or on the sidelines at high school sports events. Many normal, well-adjusted individuals do things in the heat of their kid's games that they are embarrassed about later. Recognize the danger that you, too, may succumb to this temptation, and have a plan for nipping it in the bud.

When Others Dishonor the Game

Your first responsibility as a sports parent is to model behavior that Honors the Game. But sooner or later, you will find yourself at a competition in which others are decidedly not Honoring the Game. In these situations you can play a constructive role by encouraging others to join you in Honoring the Game.

THE HIGH SCHOOL SPORTS PARENT

If a parent of a player on your team begins to berate the official, you can gently encourage them to honor the game. "Let's set a positive example for our kids and honor the game." For more on dealing with bad sideline behavior, see the case study in Chapter 9 on page 57.

Chapter 8 Take-Aways

1 Adults in high school sports often make the crucial mistake of adopting the win-at-all-cost mindset of professional sports. Recognize that the real purpose of high school sports is character development, and embrace the idea of Honoring the Game.

2 The ROOTS of Honoring the Game describe the behavior adults should teach and model: respect for Rules, Opponents, Officials, Teammates, and Self. Honoring the Game goes beyond sportsmanship, and sets a standard to inspire and motivate people to compete – win or lose – with class and grace.

3 You can teach your teen how to Honor the Game by modeling respectful behavior, seizing teachable moments when participants Honor the Game (or not), and developing a self-control routine to ensure you remain calm on the sidelines.

CHAPTER NINE

Case Studies in Second-Goal Parenting

PCA has more than a decade of experience working directly with thousands of sports parents. Through this, we've gained an intimate knowledge of some pressing issues and concerns they have as they strive to be Second-Goal Parents who support their athlete's development as a Triple-Impact Competitor.

The case studies in this chapter address some of the most frequently-asked questions, so you can apply the ideas in this book. In essence, you get to "practice" how you might use a Second-Goal focus in these situations before you encounter them with your athlete.

The heat of the moment provides a good test. The more you anticipate the kinds of situations you may encounter and think through how you want to act, the more successful you will be as a Second-Goal Parent.

Frustration is a normal and even healthy part of the high school sports experience. Dealing with tough and uncomfortable situations (a bad coach, a divided team, a disappointing season) is part of what makes high school sports such a wonderful character-building experience. The intent of these case studies isn't to suggest how parents can create a perfect environment for their kids. Rather, they suggest ways for parents to turn challenges into great learning opportunities.

To get the most from these case studies, decide (or even write) what your objective is in each situation and then what action would further that objective. Do this before reading my thoughts. Better yet, talk over the case studies with your spouse or other parents.

Keep in mind that while my thoughts on the case studies are informed by some of the best minds in high school sports, all athletes and families are different, so no one size fits all.

1. The Coach as Partner Your son has a new coach for the upcoming season. As a Second-Goal Parent, what can you do to ensure a positive relationship with the coach?

Students do better academically when they know their parents support the teacher and school. The same is certainly true for sports. Here's how you can help establish a coach-parent partnership to help your athlete have the best possible experience.

■ Contact your athlete's coach as soon as you know who it is. Introduce yourself, and let him know that you appreciate his commitment that goes way beyond the amount of time spent at practices and games. Most coaches only hear from parents when there is a problem. By establishing a positive relationship early, it will be much easier to talk with him later if a problem arises.

■ Make the coach's job easier. Attend parent meetings. Check with the coach before scheduling vacations during the season. If you can, offer to help if he ever needs volunteers. Don't say or do anything that might undermine the coach's authority. Display a positive, upbeat attitude around the coach and other parents. This will help the coach focus maximum attention on helping the players improve rather than worrying about the parents.

■ Fill the coach's Emotional Tank. When he is doing something you like, let him know, in person or by e-mail, and mention it to other parents as well. Thank him after games – especially ones when the team lost. Bring him a cup of coffee at an early morning practice. Send a thank you card in the *middle* of the season. Coaches with full E-Tanks have more to give – to the team and to your athlete.

■ Don't put your athlete in the middle between his coach and you. Never criticize the coach in front of your athlete or other parents. When parents support a coach, it is easier for an athlete to put his wholehearted effort into learning to play well, while divided loyalties make it harder for him to do his best.

■ Even if you think your teen's coach is not handling a situation well, do not share that opinion with your teen. If you conclude that something needs to be done, meet with the coach to talk about it, but not when you are upset and have trouble controlling your emotions. Observe a "cooling off" period of 24 hours. This will give you time to think about your goals and script what you want to say. Case Studies 3 and 5 have more on whether and how to talk with the coach.

■ Let the coach coach. Providing additional technical or tactical coaching can do more harm than good, especially as it may conflict with the coaches' advice. Trying to win is the responsibility of the players and coaches. You have a much more important role to play. Retain your Second-Goal focus on the life lessons your athlete learns from sports.

2. Surviving Try-Outs Your daughter is trying out for a team she really wants to make. Tryouts are coming up, and she seems nervous. As a Second-Goal Parent, what should you do?

Tryouts are tough on players and parents. They are also a great opportunity to put one's values into action. For example, if you have talked with your athlete about the virtues of being a Triple-Impact Competitor, encourage her to embody these characteristics during the try-out period. For example, if she sees a great play by another player trying out, she can compliment her on it. She can also fill E-Tanks of others who get down or make mistakes.

Every coach wants players on his team who work hard to get better, and most coaches also appreciate players who make their teammates better and who won't lose their cool in a tough situation. So, while it is good for our society to have many Triple-Impact Competitors graduating from high schools across this country, it may also help make your daughter a more desirable team member to the coach.

Given that your daughter wants to make this team so badly, she is likely going to feel nervous independent of you, but it never hurts to remind her that she doesn't have to do anything to make you proud of her. "I know you really want to make this team, and I hope you do. But it won't be the end of the world if you don't, and I certainly won't be disappointed in you if you don't."

Fear of failure often can constrict a player's performance. It may help to ask her before the try-outs begin if she can accept not making the team. Being okay with not making the team can free her up to give her best effort to make the team rather than trying to not get cut. "You may not make the team. Can you accept that you might give it your best effort and still not make the cut? If so, then you have nothing to fear."

Reinforce the ELM Tree of Mastery (see Chapter 6) by telling her that she is a winner in your books if she gives her best **E**ffort, continues to **L**earn and improve and doesn't let **M**istakes or fear of mistakes stop her. If she has learned a mistake ritual (see page 37), remind her to use it whenever she makes a mistake during the try-outs. "Remember to flush away any mistakes so you can focus on the next play."

You may want to address fear directly. "Just about all great athletes get nervous before a big competition. If you don't have a little fear, you're likely to be flat. Remember, nervous is normal."

Finally, if you have a good story about a time when you were nervous about making the cut in sports or elsewhere in life, you might want to share that story with your child, especially if it has a positive ending!

---

3. Playing Time Blues Your daughter plays less than you like. You "know" she is better than an athlete who is playing more. As a Second-Goal Parent, what should you do?

In high school sports playing time is totally at the discretion of the coach, who has much more information than any parent about relative player ability, how much effort each player is making, etc.

Although you are frustrated with your teen's playing time, she may not be. Find out. And try to do this without asking her. If you ask about whether he is frustrated by the amount of time she is on the field, you may be planting an unhelpful seed in her head.

Instead watch her. Is she excited to go to practice and games? Does she have a lot to tell you about after games? These are signs that she is engaged and not upset by her playing time.

If you come to believe that she is indeed discouraged by not playing more, you can suggest that she approach the coach to see what she can do to get more playing time. Imagine your athlete saying something like, "Coach, I'd really like to play more. Do you have any suggestions for things I can do to be able to play more?"

The coach may give her exercises to work on outside of practice. He may look for more opportunities to increase her playing time now that he knows the player is hungry to play more.

Perhaps the best thing to come from such a conversation is that your teen will have an experience talking with her coach that will be a model for dealing with supervisors and others throughout his life.

4. The Rumor Mill – Part 1 **You give your son and his teammates a ride home after the game. You hear them complaining that the coach has "favorites" who get more attention in practice and more recognition after games. What should you do with this information?**

Nothing.

Every team is a combination of competition and cooperation. Players compete for playing time while they cooperate to try to defeat the opposition. Because athletes care so much about their sport, and there is high status associated with being a starter or receiving recognition from the coach, a certain amount of complaining is normal even on a good team with a positive, effective coach. Let it go.

The Rumor Mill — Part 2 You give your son and his teammates a ride home after the game. You hear some very troubling information that seems to indicate that the coach may be abusing a player. What should you do with this information?

Unlike the previous case, you have a responsibility to investigate further to ensure no player is being harmed. However, you have no proof, so proceed with extreme caution.

■ Talk with your son to get a better picture of the situation. "I couldn't help overhearing in the car that Coach Jones is pretty upset with Derek. What more can you tell me about this?"

■ Seek confirmation of what you heard. You might ask a parent you trust to not feed the rumor mill if he or she has heard anything along these lines. Whether or not something unacceptable has happened, adding fuel to the gossip fire does no one any good.

■ If you find reason to worry about the situation, you need to decide whether to talk with the coach first or go directly to a supervisor (athletic director or principal). In general, it is a good to talk with the coach about a problem before going over his head; however, if there is indication of abusive or criminal behavior, you may be better off going to the athletic director or principal directly.

■ Script your key points before hand to help you say what you want in a non-confrontational, constructive way. Explain what you have heard and why you are concerned. Listen to the response and then, if needed, decide what more you need to do.

This is a tough call with no absolute rule of thumb to guide you. The one certainty is that if there is evidence of a coach abusing a player, you have to take it seriously and report it to the proper officials, likely the athletic director and principal. It is better to err on the side of being too careful about something like this than to let it slide.

5. The Ineffective Coach Your son's coach is ineffective. He is occasionally late for practice, often appears disorganized, and doesn't command the respect of the athletes. You think the athletes deserve a more effective coach. As a Second-Goal Parent, what should you do?

The Hippocratic Oath doctors take says, "Do no harm." Doctors do nothing if they think they might make things worse. The chances of you improving this situation by offering suggestions to the coach are very small, while the chances of making things worse are high. Do no harm. Stay out of this.

Here's what you can do.

■ Write on a piece of paper your suggestions for how you think your athlete's coach should handle the team. Put it in an envelope. On the outside of the envelope, write "If I were the coach." Put it in a safe place. Whatever you do, don't give the suggestions to the coach.

■ If the school has an evaluation mechanism to get input from parents, take advantage of it to share your feedback.

Let your athlete have his own experience with the coach. Having a sub-par coach isn't a tragedy. Your teen will have talented and untalented supervisors in his life, and learning to deal with both kinds is a great life lesson.

6. The Bad Call A bad call goes against your school's team in a really important game. Another parent from your teen's school goes nuts and loudly berates the official. What should you do?

There are two objectives worth considering in this situation. A good minimum objective is to make sure that you behave in a way that Honors the Game. A worthy, more ambitious goal would be to help defuse the situation with the verbally abusive parent.

Here's what you can do:

■   Bite your tongue. If you have to turn away or even walk away from the sidelines to maintain your composure, then do it. If you have a short fuse in situations like this, use your Self-Control Ritual to make sure you Honor the Game. (Don't know what this is? See page 49.)

Recognize that you are not an independent agent in this situation. You represent your teen and her school. Other people will associate your behavior with the school, so you need to Honor the Game no matter what to avoid giving your teen's school a black eye.

■   Help calm the abusive parent. It is much easier to do this if your school or coach has already made Honoring the Game part of the team's culture. If so, use that vocabulary now.

In some cases you can get your point across with a light touch: "Hey, none of us want to go home and have our kids give us grief about how we acted tonight."

■   Whatever you do, don't do anything to make the situation worse. Don't invade the other parent's personal space, or threaten him in any way. If you don't think you can be a calming influence, it's better to stay out of it.

■   Unless you are in an extremely rare situation where the official is biased against your athlete's team, calls will go both ways. You can defuse tension by calling attention to good calls that officials make as well as bad calls that go against the other team (which are usually ignored while calls against "our" team are held close and picked over like a scab). "Wow, that helped our team, but it seemed like a really bad call. I guess the bad calls are going both ways today."

■   Make a point of thanking officials after the game. This may be difficult if the official made calls that hurt your athlete's team and even more challenging if the calls led to a loss, but I bet you can do it. "I'd like to thank you for officiating today. I know you don't hear this much, so I just wanted to express my appreciation. Thank you." Then enjoy seeing the officials look grateful or amazed (or both)! And feel good about your ability to Honor the Game under trying circumstances.

Your behavior can serve as a powerful model for Honoring the Game both for your budding Triple-Impact Competitor and for other parents.

7. The Club vs. High School Dilemma Your son plays for an elite soccer team. The coach wants him to quit other sports, including his high school soccer team, to play exclusively with the club team. As a Second-Goal Parent, what should you do?

I start with a bias. I loved playing for my high school team. I was proud to wear green and white and represent West Fargo (ND) High School, and playing with my friends was great. I am sad when I hear of elite athletes passing up their high school team to play exclusively for a club team. So I tend to encourage athletes to try to keep playing for their high school team if they can.

I also understand that people get better by competing against opponents who push them to be their best. Some athletes may be better served by playing for a club team if that is the best or only place they can get the necessary competition. However, it is important to realize that your son's club coach may have an agenda that doesn't align perfectly with what is best for your son.

Many professional athletes did not specialize until quite late. Furthermore, they often say that playing multiple sports helped them when they did specialize, often not until college.

If you have not already used the 100-Points Exercise (see Chapter 4) for a conversation about your son's goals in sports, this would be a good time to do so. After discussing the various goals he has in sports, you might ask him to sort them into two columns: "Best Achieved on High School team" and "Best Achieved on Club Team." Then you can have him consider which team (club or high school) offers the best opportunity to achieve each goal.

If your son decides he wants to concentrate on his club team after considering the advantages and disadvantages, it could be a great thing for him. But it makes sense to do so after thinking through the advantages and disadvantages of each, including playing for both teams.

8. Ouch! Dealing With Injuries Your soccer-playing daughter has joined the walking wounded. She has played soccer pretty much year-round for the past several years, alternating high school and club teams. She was injured again recently, and the doctor says it will be weeks before she can play again. As a Second-Goal Parent, what can you do to help your daughter?

There are two tricky issues embedded in this situation. Let's unpack them.

- First, understand that way too many young athletes are experiencing repetitive stress injuries from overuse. The drive to improve, to be great, to please one or more coaches, or to attract attention from college scouts can result in an out-of-control situation with severe physical consequences for high school athletes at a time when they are already vulnerable because of rapid growth.

In the made-for-TV movie of Joan Ryan's important and troubling book, *Little Girls in Pretty Boxes,* a mom has uprooted her gymnast-daughter and herself from their family to allow the daughter to train with a highly regarded professional coach. At the end of the film, the mom confronts the coach about his pushing the daughter to resume practice before the mom feels her daughter has recovered from an injury. The mom tells the coach that he has a responsibility to make sure her daughter is healthy. The coach responds, "No. My job is to make her a champion. Her health is your responsibility."

It is not reasonable to expect a teenage athlete to have the long-term perspective of an adult. Most athletes will almost always say they want to play more rather than less. For athletes with a highly evolved sense of competitiveness, it may seem a sign of weakness to admit they are hurting. That's where parents come in. You may have to act as a governor on your athlete's desire to compete. And on your own conscious or subconscious dreams for her.

You may also have to deal with a coach who, though well-intentioned, encourages your daughter to rejoin the team before she is fully healed.

Gear up to resist the pressures and ensure that once she is healed, you don't let your daughter ever again play so much soccer that her health and her ultimate future in the game may be put in jeopardy.

■ Next is helping your daughter cope with being out of competition for an extended period of time, which may be a challenge for her.

Let your daughter know that injuries are a part of being an elite athlete and that she has a terrific opportunity to learn to manage her reaction to injuries starting with this one. Persistence, resilience, and a positive attitude are great helps in coming back from an injury (as well as for so many things she'll want to accomplish in life).

Encourage her to focus her energy on working her rehabilitation routine just as she would in practice. You can help make it a positive experience, perhaps charting her progress and celebrating "small wins" each step of the way. You might point out that her rehab plan could serve as a model for accomplishing other things unrelated to injuries.

When I was sidelined with a broken rib on my right side as a high school basketball player, I spent hours dribbling and shooting with my left hand. I also learned to open my locker and brush my teeth with my left hand. If your daughter can work on an area where she could improve without compromising her recovery, it might be a big morale booster for her.

Ask her coach to can find ways for her to feel part of the team during her injury. He might have her analyze videotape of future opponents, mentor younger players, chart statistics during games, or even help with fundraising. She might also serve as team journalist writing stories about the team for the school paper or the team's web site. PCA has developed a terrific tool called Positive Charting (find it at www.positivecoach.org), which she could use to note the positive things her teammates are doing as a way to help them improve, per Level 2 of the Triple-Impact Competitor model (making teammates better).

As she gets closer to healing, your daughter will likely want to begin playing. Resist the temptation to let her back on the field before she is ready. It helps to have a medical opinion from a qualified individual who has no interest in her team's success so you can rely on his or her advice.

Handled properly, your daughter may look back on her rehab as a positive step in her career as a soccer player.

9. Quitting Time? **Your son is not enjoying his chosen sport any more. He has played for years and excels at it. But now he appears burned out and has even mentioned he wants to quit. As a Second-Goal Parent, what should you do?**

Peter Benson, author of *Sparks*, a landmark book on teen motivation, says: "Sparks illuminate a young person's life and give it energy and purpose." Helping teens find their spark and encouraging it is an important role for parents, which may be hard if you are emotionally attached to your son competing in his sport, while it no longer sparks him.

Try to disengage yourself from your hopes and dreams for your son as an athlete. This is about what's best for him, and if he feels he needs to please you, it will be much harder for him to figure out what is best for him.

Juliet Thompson Hochman, a member of the 1988 U.S. Olympic Rowing Team, shared a conversation she had with her father the summer after her first year at Harvard. She was away from family, teammates, and coaches working out but feeling lonely and discouraged. She talked to her father who reminded her that she could quit rowing if that's what she wanted.

Juliet might have been expecting her dad to pressure her, to talk her into sticking with her workouts. Instead, he reminded her that she could change her situation. She thought about what she wanted to do and realized that she wanted to excel in rowing for herself, not to please her father or anyone else. She rededicated herself, made the U.S. national team the following year, and competed in the Olympics in Seoul.

Whether to quit or not may seem like a "forever" decision to your son, but it doesn't have to be. He can decide to take a break, even skip a season of competition, without that meaning that he is quitting the sport for good. If he takes some time off, he may find he misses it, or he may feel relieved to be away. He won't know unless he does take a break.

So, take some of the pressure off the decision. Decisions made under pressure are often not as good as those where we give ourselves time to figure out the best course of action.

Here are some questions you might ask to get a conversation going:

- Is this a recent feeling, or have you felt this way for a while?
- Does this feel like temporary burnout or something deeper?
- Do you think taking some time off would help?
- What is it about playing your sport that feels different now?
- If you do quit, are there other activities that you'd like to get involved with?

Then listen carefully to what he says.

At some point it may be useful to help frame the decision with what I call the Five-Year Question. "How do you think you will feel five years from now if you keep playing? If you take a break? If you quit?"

It also may help for your son to "live with" each decision for a while. For a week he could live with the idea that he will gut it out and keep playing. When he gets up in the morning and he realizes that he is going to keep playing, how does he feel? Then a week living with the decision to quit playing the sport. Again, how does he feel? Doing this for several days at a time may clarify what the best decision is for him.

Ask him to consider the idea of "responsible quitting." If your son quits in mid-season, how will that impact his teammates and coach? What could he do to honor his commitment to the team while also taking care of his own needs? What would it mean for him to quit in a responsible way? Often this means giving notice, so the coach, for example, could develop another player to take over your son's role on the team.

Also note that burnout with a sport can accompany other more serious problems, such as stress, depression, social problems, or eating disorders. Your conversations with your son around his sport may lead to important information about whether this is part of a bigger problem, which might not have surfaced otherwise.

I grew up with the idea that it was not okay to quit something I had started. I even felt that I should finish any book I started reading, regardless of how bad it was. But I now see how foolish this was. Time spent with a bad book is time I can't spend reading a great book. If your son continues with a sport that is not rewarding to him, this is time he is not able to spend doing something rewarding, or exploring other potentially meaningful things he can do with his time.

10. The Next Level: Playing in College? **Your daughter shows potential to play beyond high school. She has been approached by the local community college coach and also has received mail from several Division I and II programs. She is flattered by this attention but doesn't know how to manage the choices she faces. As a Second-Goal Parent, how can you help her?**

Decisions about college are more complex than they used to be. Add in the potential for an athletic scholarship and it can boggle the mind of a teen athlete and her family. You can help your athlete deal with this complexity and turn it into a great preparation for other complex decisions in her life.

First, recognize that an athletic scholarship is a means to a bigger end – getting a great education that will serve your daughter the rest of her life. Having college coaches interested in their child can be a big high for parents who love basking in their child's reflected glory, so try to keep your feet on the ground so you can look out for your daughter's best interests.

Start the conversation by asking what your daughter thinks she might like to study in college. Suggest that the ideal college might be one that combines the kind of academic environment she wants with an athletic experience she'll enjoy. You might ask, "Would you be happy at this college if they dropped your sport or if you decided not to play?"

The recruiting process can be stressful for high school athletes because it seems so overwhelming. Breaking it down can help restore a sense that it is manageable. Together develop an initial list of no more than ten to fifteen colleges that seem to provide both the academic and athletic experience that your daughter would benefit from.

Have her call and e-mail the coaches of the programs she is interested in. After talking with them, if there is mutual interest, have her put together a recruiting package, including a photo, resume, and highlight DVD. Mail it to the coach with a personalized cover letter.

When coaches from schools not on your list contact your daughter, do them a favor. Let them know she is isn't interested in considering them so they can turn their attention to other recruits.

Athletes can be star struck at the possibility of playing at a Division I school when the best combination of academics and sports may be at a Division II or III school (which only offers academic or need-based scholarships). Too many college athletes transfer or quit because they choose a college at a level above where they would be happy.

There is also some blocking and tackling that needs to be done. Become familiar with NCAA clearinghouse rules at www.ncaa.org. See a school counselor to make sure your athlete is taking the classes needed for the schools she is considering. Enlist the help of the coach, who may have experience with scholarship athletes. And, consider talking to college athletes who have graduated from your teen's high school.

Finally, recognize that turning down athletic scholarships is an option. As we saw in Chapter 4, college athletics is a big commitment. Athletes sometimes feel like they have a full-time job on top of their academic schedule. Make sure your daughter understands how much work it is and that she is committed to it. If not, she may be much happier and better off by attending college without playing sports.

Positive Coaching Alliance's Big Mission

Positive Coaching Alliance has a huge mission: *To transform youth sports so sports can transform youth.* Sports provide an endless procession of teachable moments that can be used by adults to develop great people. But too often it just doesn't happen.

Our mission will be achieved when the prevailing models in youth and high school sports are:

- **Double-Goal Coaches** who use sports to teach life lessons as they prepare their teams for success on the scoreboard

- **Triple-Impact Competitors** who make themselves, their teammates, and the game better

- **Second-Goal Parents** who concentrate on their child's character development while letting athletes and coaches focus on the first goal of winning on the scoreboard

Imagine what the experience of high school sports will be like when coaches, parents, and athletes embrace these roles and play them to the hilt! There are few things as promising for our society as developing teams full of Triple-Impact Competitors – for their impact on the field and in life long afterward.

If you like what PCA is trying to do, here are some ways you can spread the PCA Movement so, **together**, we can transform the culture of youth sports!

1) Become a Second-Goal Parent. Use the ideas and tools in this book to help your child have a great experience with sports. You will also serve as a role model to other sports parents to emulate.

2) Spread the word. Tell people about your experience as a Second-Goal Parent. The more ideas like Honoring the Game, the ELM Tree of Mastery, and the Emotional Tank are discussed, the more people will use them to help their children.

3) Promote Double-Goal Coaching. Ask if your teen's coach has been trained and certified as a Double-Goal Coach. If so, thank him. If not, refer him to PCA's on-line Double-Goal Coach workshop at www.positivecoach.org. You might consider investing in your teen's coach by paying the on-line workshop fee as a gift.

4) Get your organizations involved. Ask your teen's school and youth sports organizations if they have earned the "PCA Seal of Commitment," which signifies that every coach in the organization is a trained and certified Double-Goal Coach. If not, refer them to the PCA web site (www.positivecoach.org) or our toll-free number 1-866-725-0024.

5) Reward great coaching. Nominate a great youth or high school coach for PCA's national Double-Goal Coach Award. Find out how at www.positivecoach.org.

6) Become a "PCA Champion." Promote the PCA Movement in your community. Contact pca@positivecoach.org to find out more.

7) Stay connected to PCA. Sign up for PCA Connector, our e-newsletter, at www.positivecoach.org for sports parenting tips and updates. Express your opinions through PCA's blogs on our web site.

8) Support the PCA Movement. You can make a tax-exempt donation at www.positivecoach.org or by mail at Positive Coaching Alliance, 1001 N. Rengstorff Avenue, Mountain View, CA 94303.

9) Give PCA away. Buy copies of this book for other sports parents you know. Coaching books such as *The Double-Goal Coach* or *Positive Coaching in a Nutshell* would be great for coaches you know.

Thank you for your support for transforming youth sports so sports can transform youth!

What are YOUR goals for playing high school sports?

_____ Become a good athlete

_____ Learn to play the sport

_____ Learn teamwork as part of a team

_____ Win

_____ Gain increased self-confidence

_____ Learn to deal with defeat

_____ Physical fitness

_____ Learn "life lessons"

_____ Have fun

_____ Make friends

_____ Earn a varsity letter

_____ Earn a college scholarship

_____ Other (specify: _____)

_____ Other (specify: _____)

_100_ TOTAL